PAUL
GAUGUIN

PAUL GAUGUIN

MARIA COSTANTINO

BARNES
&NOBLE
BOOKS
NEW YORK

This edition published by
Barnes and Noble Inc.,
by arrangement with Brompton
Books Corporation

Produced by Brompton Books
Corporation
15 Sherwood Place
Greenwich, CT 06830

ISBN 1-56619-464-4

Printed in Spain

PAGE 1: *Four Breton Women*, 1886,
Bayerischen Staatsgemäldesammlungen, Munich

PAGE 2: *Vahine no te Vi (Woman
with a Mango)*, 1892, Baltimore
Museum of Art

CONTENTS

INTRODUCTION

Paul Gauguin was born in Paris on 7 June 1848 at 56 rue Notre Dame de Lorette. His father, Clovis, was a journalist from Orléans; Aline, his mother, was the daughter of lithographer André Chazal and Flora Moscosa, better known as Flora Tristan, a Peruvian woman writer and socialist agitator. At the time of Paul's birth Paris was in turmoil: the June Revolt of 1848, by workers in protest against the closing of workshops by the newly-elected conservative National Assembly, was being bloodily suppressed in the streets of Paris. The political climate of the time jeopardized Clovis Gauguin's position as editor of the *National* newspaper, particularly after Louis Napoléon was elected president. Events came to a head following Louis Napoléon's *coup d'état* in December 1851, and Clovis Gauguin took his family into exile in Peru.

During the crossing of the Straits of Magellan between South America and Tierra del Fuego, Clovis unfortunately died from an aneurism and was buried at Porta Famina. His widow and two young children, Paul and Mary, continued the journey and landed at Lima, where they were to live with Flora Tristan's uncle Dom Pio Tristan y Moscoso, a former viceroy of Peru. The sights and exotic atmosphere of South America were to remain with Gauguin all his life, predisposing him toward the tropics. Four years later, however, the Gauguin family returned to France, to Orléans, where Paul was enrolled as a day pupil at a local school run by priests. Later he entered the Lycée, where it was hoped he would qualify for the naval training school. In the end Gauguin shipped out as a navigating cadet on board the *Lusitano*, which traded between Le Havre on the English

LEFT: *Gauguin in Front of his Easel*, 1885. This introspective self-portrait dates from the year after Gauguin followed his wife and children back to her native Copenhagen, soon after his decision to leave stockbroking and become a full-time artist. It was an unhappy and isolated, but extremely productive, period for him; he painted about 50 canvases in 1885, compared with no more than a dozen in any of the preceding years.

LEFT: Pissarro: *Portrait of Gauguin* and Gauguin: *Portrait of Pissarro*, c.1883. Gauguin's early work was much influenced by the older Impressionist painter, and in 1881 he joined Pissarro at his home in Pontoise and worked under his guidance.

Channel coast and the Brazilian seaport Rio de Janeiro. In the course of this first voyage, Gauguin was dazzled by the beauty of the bay of Rio and not a little beguiled by the stories told to him by the second mate, who as a cabin boy had been wrecked in some archipelago of Oceania, the central and south Pacific, where he claimed he had lived for two years in Paradise. These stories and his own love of the sea were to have a significant influence much later, when Gauguin left France for Tahiti.

Following his cadetship Gauguin enlisted in the French navy, and in February 1868 he shipped out as a third class hand and stoker on board the *Jérome Napoléon*. In April 1871 Gauguin received ten months' renewable leave, and while in Paris he decided to give up his career at sea. His mother Aline had just died at Saint-Cloud, where she had been a neighbor and friend of the rich and influential Arosa family. Thanks to Gustave Arosa, who was appointed legal guardian to the Gauguin children, Paul secured a clerk's job with the Paris stockbroking company of Bertin in the rue Lafitte, where he remained for eleven years. Having swiftly mastered the intricacies of the stock market, Gauguin began his own speculating. A fellow painter, Emile Schuffenecker (1851-1934), who also worked at Bertin, claimed that Gauguin's successes in the market earned him forty thousand francs in a single year.

At around this time Gauguin and Schuffenecker began to study painting in the evenings at a large, informally-run studio, the Atelier Colarossi. Gauguin's interest in painting was undoubtedly fired by two major influences. The first was the considerable collection amassed by his guardian Arosa of contemporary paintings by artists such as Courbet, Corot and Delacroix. Secondly, at some point in the early 1870s, Gauguin was introduced to Camille Pissarro (1830-

1903), one of the guiding forces behind the first Impressionist exhibition, which showed works by Monet, Renoir, Cézanne, Sisley, Morisot and Degas among others. Following Arosa's example, Gauguin began investing in works by members of the impressionist circle. This was partly for financial security, but it is also possible that Gauguin was using the paintings as a means of self-instruction. By the mid 1880s his collection included works by a number of Impressionists, including Renoir, Sisley and Degas, several by Pissarro, one by Manet and six paintings by Cézanne, which Gauguin regarded so highly that even when he was short of money he refused to sell them.

Gauguin seemed in the 1870s to have settled down to the stable life of a Paris stockbroker. In 1873 he married Mette Sofie Gad, a Danish girl, the daughter of a Lutheran minister, who was introduced to him at Arosa's home. A 'Sunday painter', Gauguin's first work bearing a definite date, of 1873, is a landscape owing much to the work of Corot, which Gauguin would have seen in Arosa's collection, and to that of his now close companion, Camille Pissarro.

By 1876 Gauguin was in close contact with several of the 'Indépendants': Cézanne, Guillaumin, and even Manet, who encouraged him to continue his painting. Yet despite Gauguin's interest in the Indépendants, he sent a landscape in the same year to the official Salon exhibition. It was only in 1879 that Gauguin first exhibited with the Impressionists. He was listed in the catalog as lending three landscapes by Pissarro, but a late invitation from Degas to show his own paintings with the group meant that Gauguin's name was not included among the contributing artists. From his own works Gauguin submitted not a painting, but a marble bust of his eldest son Emile.

RIGHT: Cézanne: *The Castle at Médan*, 1880. Cézanne was also a formative influence on the young Gauguin, with his successful combination, as here, of a more systematic structuring of the picture, by means of coherently grouped sloping brushstrokes, together with the freshness of outdoor painting espoused by the Impressionists.

The following year, 1880, Gauguin exhibited with the Impressionists again, submitting eight works, one of which was another marble bust, this time of his wife Mette. In 1881 the dealer Durand-Ruel bought three of Gauguin's paintings, and at the Impressionist exhibition that year he showed eight paintings and two sculptures. It was at this, the sixth group show, that Gauguin received his first positive reviews, from the critic and novelist Joris-Karl Huysmans for the *Study of a Nude*. Huysmans admired its realism, and also described a small statuette of a figure in painted wood called *Lady Walking* as 'gothically modern', but remarked that, with his landscapes, Gauguin was still having trouble 'escaping' from the influence of Pissarro. In 1882, when Gauguin next exhibited with the Impressionists, his submissions were his most ambitious to date, comprising

a number of landscapes, four still lifes, several figure studies (including a bust of his son Clovis) and three paintings of his children. Huysmans, however, considered that Gauguin had not made any real progress.

The next year, 1883, marked a turning point in Gauguin's career. The romantic mythologizers of his life would have it that suddenly, without a word of warning (even to his wife), Gauguin announced 'From now on I paint every day,' and promptly resigned his position at Bertin, sacrificing all for his art. More realistically, it would appear that Gauguin lost his job as an indirect result of the collapse of the stock exchange at the beginning of 1882. Now faced with a growing family – a fifth child was expected in 1883 – and doubtful financial security in the form of a collection of contemporary art, he had to consider making a living as a full-time artist.

Having sold much of his collection at a loss, Gauguin left Paris and moved his family to Rouen, where it was hoped they could live more cheaply. The following year, however, Mette Gauguin, who preferred a more comfortable lifestyle, took the new baby and their daughter Aline to Copenhagen. Gauguin followed in November, bringing the other children and the remnants of his prized collection of paintings, most of which were destined to stay in Denmark and to be gradually sold off by Mette whenever the family became short of money. The period in Copenhagen does not appear to have been a particularly happy one. Gauguin worked as an agent for a French tarpaulin company, despite his lack of Danish, while his wife gave French lessons. Financial pressures, along with his antipathy toward the Danes in general and his in-laws in particular, as well as his isolation from the artistic climate of Paris, no doubt put a great strain on the family.

In spite of this, Gauguin's artistic output was prolific: in 1885 alone he painted 50 canvases. His work received little critical attention in Copenhagen, however, and in June 1885, accompanied by his six-year-old son Clovis,

Gauguin returned to Paris. At the eighth and final Impressionist exhibition in the following year, Gauguin was one of the main contributors with nineteen paintings, the majority of which were landscapes. These were exhibited alongside the works of newcomers to the group, including Georges Seurat (1859-91) and Paul Signac (1863-1935).

Still hard-pressed for cash, Gauguin decided in July 1886 to leave Paris and spend the summer in Brittany. He settled at Pont-Aven, a small port four miles from the sea, staying at the Pension Gloanec. Various contemporary guidebooks recommended parts of Brittany to artists for its climate, suitable for *plein-air* painting, its landscape and its inhabitants. Gauguin was later to write to his friend Schuffenecker: 'I feel something savage, primitive here.'

It was in Brittany that Gauguin first met Emile Bernard, a young painter who had walked from Paris to Pont-Aven and who was later to work closely with Gauguin. This first stay in Brittany, however, produced little noticeable change in Gauguin's work. As Bernard was to write:

My stay at Pont-Aven passed without our feeling in touch with each other; we did not even talk, although we were neighbors at table.

When winter came, Gauguin returned to Paris. In Montmartre he met Vincent van Gogh, newly arrived from Holland, but the decisive exchanges between the two artists were still some way off. Drawing on his experiences in Brittany as subject matter for his work in Paris, Gauguin painted *Four Breton Women* (1886) and ventured into the medium of ceramics, in which he used simplified Breton imagery.

The following spring, the longstanding call of the sea and a desire for a simpler and more 'savage' way of life led Gauguin to quit Europe. In April 1887, Gauguin left 'the poor man's desert' of Paris for Panama, accompanied by a painter friend Charles Laval. When the pair arrived a month later, their hopes for travelling on to Tobago were thwarted by a lack of funds.

LEFT: *Portrait Bust of Mette Gauguin*, 1879.

BELOW: Monet: *Impression Setting Sun*, 1872, shown at the Fourth Impressionist exhibition.

RIGHT: Photograph of the Pension Gloanec, Pont-Aven, with Gauguin seated in the front row and a number of local women in traditional Breton dress.

While Laval worked on portrait commissions, Gauguin, refusing to compromise what he believed was his artistic integrity, worked for fifteen days as a laborer constructing the Panama Canal.

After being laid off Gauguin, with Laval, went to Martinique, a French possession since the seventeenth century. Here he at last got down to some painting and began to explore the forms and colors of the tropics that were to obsess him until the end of his life. This stay in Martinique marked the first decisive steps in Gauguin's career as an independent artist.

Nevertheless life on the island was hard for the two men. Both were suffering from dysentery and malaria, and Laval's condition became so acute that he attempted suicide. Gauguin's dream of living like a native was killing them.

In January 1888 Gauguin and Laval were back in Paris, homeless and penniless. Fortunately for Gauguin, help was at hand in the form of his old friend Schuffenecker. Before he had left for Panama, Gauguin had left the few paintings he most valued in his friend's care, at his small house near the Place d'Enfer. Staying with Schuffenecker, Gauguin now made the acquaintance of the ceramicist Chaplet, who taught him the techniques of earthenware and earthenware

decoration. Also through Schuffenecker, Gauguin was introduced to the painter Daniel de Monfreid, who became a regular correspondent and devoted mediator when Gauguin was in Tahiti.

While in Martinique, Gauguin had been diligent in sending back to Paris his completed paintings, and a number of these and his new Paris ceramics were exhibited in a Paris gallery toward the end of 1887. Here they were admired by Vincent van Gogh and his brother Theo. During the following year Theo bought a number of Gauguin's works, and in the summer of 1888 he offered Gauguin a regular monthly income of 150 francs in exchange for one painting if Gauguin would join Vincent in Arles in the south of France. At the beginning of 1888 Gauguin had returned to Brittany and remained there until October, when he left for Arles. In Brittany he was joined again by Emile Bernard, whom he had met briefly two years earlier, and through him Gauguin became acquainted with the latest literary theories of the Symbolists Jean Moréas and Albert Aurier, who stressed the role of the imagination in seeking to convey a vision of reality. Gauguin's 'synthesis' was taking shape and he was beginning his most important works of that year, such as *The Vision After the Sermon*. In trying to convey the effects of a religious experience on a group of peasant women. Gauguin abandoned traditional western perspective and naturalistic color, rendering the clothes of the figures as flat blocks of color.

Meanwhile, in Arles, van Gogh had been preparing for Gauguin's arrival for some time; he envisaged a stimulating and productive artistic community. The two painters often drew on the same subject matter; for example, van Gogh painted *The Night Café*, Gauguin the *Night Café at Arles* and in December the pair traveled around the coast up to Montpellier, where they visited the Bruyas collection housed in the museum there. Later Gauguin was to translate one of the Courbet paintings he had seen in the museum, *Bonjour Monsieur Courbet*, into his own *Bonjour Monsieur Gauguin* (1889).

A few days after the trip van Gogh's mental health, which had already led him to alternating extremes of violence and affection toward Gauguin, deteriorated further. He threatened his friend with murder and later in the same evening resorted to self-mutilation, cutting off part of his own ear. With van Gogh hospitalized, Gauguin returned with Theo van Gogh to Paris.

Early in 1889 Gauguin set off once again for Pont-Aven, where he began planning his most ambitious project: an exhibition to capitalize on the crowds of spectators expected in Paris to enjoy the Exposition Universelle, in celebration of the centenary of the French Revolution. Underneath the newly constructed Eiffel Tower, the Palais des Beaux-Arts was to display the work of Salon artists, including paintings by now-acceptable artists such as Manet, Cézanne, Monet and Pissarro. Gauguin chose to distance himself from the official Salon, however, by exhibiting at an alternative

ABOVE: *Vase with Breton Girls*, 1886-87. After his return to Paris from Brittany in autumn 1886, Gauguin experimented with the medium of ceramics, simplifying and paring down his Breton imagery to suit it.

LEFT: Van Gogh: *The Night Café*, 1888. In contrast to Gauguin's version of this subject (pages 58-59), van Gogh evoked a mood of menace by means of rushing diagonals and simplified colors.

RIGHT: Bernard: *Portrait of My Sister Madeleine*. 1888. Emile Bernard and Gauguin worked together in Brittany during much of 1888, and Gauguin fell in love with Bernard's younger sister Madeleine, who had accompanied her brother and was a willing model for both artists.

venue. Schuffenecker had persuaded Monsieur Volpini, who owned the Café des Arts near the Palais, to display a number of works between May and July. Eight artists of the 'Impressionist and Synthetist Group' were represented: Schuffenecker, Bernard, Laval, Louis Anquetin, Louis Roy, Léon Foche, George Nemo and Paul Gauguin himself, who between them showed a total of 100 works, 17 of which were by Gauguin.

For the public and critics, as Maurice Denis later recorded, this exhibition was one of the most shocking and hilarious spectacles of the Exposition. Meanwhile Gauguin had become interested in the fair's 'Javanese Village', where the Hindu dancing girls had caught his eye. The idea of another trip to the tropics was to preoccupy him for some time. In the summer of 1890 he wrote to Bernard:

What I want to do is set up a studio in the tropics . . . I can buy a hut of the kind you saw at the Exposition Universelle.

For the next two years Gauguin spent his time planning his 'escape' from France but, after hesitating between Madagasgar and Tahiti, he settled on Brittany! Pont-Aven was now far too touristy for his liking, however, so Gauguin went out to the end of Cape Finistère, to the empty beaches of Le Pouldu, where his Brittany period was to reach its climax. He wrote to his wife, 'I live like a peasant under the name "Sauvage".' At Le Pouldu Gauguin worked closely with Paul Sérusier, Meyer de Haan and his old friend Charles Laval. During the period summer 1889 to November 1890 he painted some of his finest works, including *Self-Portrait with Halo* and *Yellow Christ*.

With a number of paintings completed, Gauguin returned to Paris in 1890. There he had developed something of a reputation, particularly among male artists who no doubt envied his lifestyle, conveniently unencumbered with familial responsibilities. Homeless as usual, he again lodged with Schuffenecker before moving

LEFT: Bernard: *The Buckwheat Harvest*, 1888. Through Bernard, Gauguin was introduced to the latest literary theories, including Symbolism. The brilliant red and simplified line in this work may well have influenced Gauguin's change of direction at this time, particularly in *The Vision after the Sermon* (pages 50-51), a key work of the year.

to a small hotel in the rue Delambre and sharing Monfreid's studio.

Had he chosen to stay in Paris and set up as a grand painter of the Symbolist movement, Gauguin's success would no doubt have been assured. Restless as usual, however, he was consumed by the idea of returning to the tropics. In order to raise money to finance his proposed trip, he held a sale of his paintings at the public auction house, the Hôtel Drouot. On 23 February 1891, 30 of Gauguin's paintings were sold, realizing 10,000 francs. After seeing his wife and children in Copenhagen for what proved to be the last time, Gauguin left France on 4 April on the first of his trips to Tahiti.

Gauguin was neither the only nor the first artist who attempted to 'break' with 'the west' and sail off to the South Seas. In 1888 Robert Louis Stevenson had set out for Polynesia, while 50 years earlier Herman Melville had made a similar voyage, which he used in *Moby Dick* (1851). Furthermore, if Gauguin had gone to Tahiti in order to escape civilization and to return to a simpler way of life, he would have been greatly disappointed. By the time he arrived in Papeete in June 1891, the capital of French Polynesia was a European shanty town, with many Tahitians converted to Christianity, attending missionary schools and wearing westernized clothing. Few of the old religious beliefs were in evidence, and the hoped-for idols and rituals were almost completely gone. Gauguin was in fact forced to invent a native artistic tradition for himself from a number of sources: photographs and drawings of Javanese temples, Japanese prints, and religious artifacts from Brittany.

Furthermore, he remained in contact with Paris, receiving regular packages from France and subscribing to journals in which were reproduced illustrations on which he freely drew.

In 1892 a colonial lawyer lent Gauguin a copy of J A Moerenhout's 1837 publication *Voyages aux Iles du Grand Océan*, which dealt with the geography, politics, language, religion, customs and costumes of Polynesia. From this Gauguin copied large sections into his notebook, which he called *Ancien Culte Mahorie* and illustrated with original watercolors. This was subsequently to become the basis for his most important literary work, *Noa Noa*. Rather than documenting the realities of late-nineteenth century life in Tahiti in his paintings, Gauguin's images depicted a highly selective, personal vision of the island, based largely on historical material.

Gauguin's original plan for seeking patronage in Tahiti had been upset by the death of the King, Pomare V, and he was subsequently forced to look to portraiture as a means of making a living. Although he wrote to Mette that he had been overwhelmed with requests for portraits, he seems in fact to have secured only one commission, the portrait of Suzanne Bambridge. A few months after his arrival in Papeete, he moved around the coast to Mataiea, 25 miles south of the capital and in a less colonized area of the island. With him was the first of his young native girl companions, Titi; soon after she left him, he 'married' Tehamana, in a native ceremony. A thirteen-year-old girl who was to bear his child, Tehamana was also to be the subject of a number of paintings and was immortalized in *Noa Noa*.

RIGHT: This photograph of Papeete, dating from around 1900, is evidence of the degree of colonialization and 'civilization' – including street lamps – of which Gauguin complained.

The work Gauguin sent back to Paris did not sell as well as he had expected. When he left Paris he had 9000 francs; eighteen months later. in spite of his so-called 'simple life', his money was running out. In the last months of 1892, he made increasingly desperate pleas to Paris and Copenhagen for funds, and tried several times to be repatriated. In May 1893 he was finally granted a passage back to Marseille, and left Tahiti at the beginning of June.

Gauguin was eager to get back to Paris, where he believed (as he had written to Monfreid): 'a whole troop of my youthful followers is making a noise and thriving . . .' But there was no-one to meet him on arrival and his return to Paris went unnoticed. Borrowing money from a

woman shopkeeper and linen from Monfreid, Gauguin rented a small studio in the rue de la Grande-Chaumière. There he began arranging for a one-man show of his Tahitian paintings at Durand-Ruel's gallery in November 1893. At this exhibition Gauguin showed over 40 paintings. including *Nafea Faa Ipoipo? (When will you marry?)*, *Under the Pandanus* and *The House of the Maori*. He had hoped to repeat the success of the sale held at the Hôtel Drouot two years earlier, but prices were higher and fewer than ten paintings were sold. although Gauguin himself described it as a critical success.

Out of the blue came news of an inheritance from his uncle. Isidore Gauguin. The bequest of 13,000 francs

LEFT: *Self-portrait for Carrière*, probably 1888 and 1895, is an intimate self-portrait intended for a fellow-artist.

enabled him to move to more comfortable surroundings in the rue Vercingétorix. Living with him was his latest girlfriend, a Singalese who went by the name of 'Annah the Javanese'. The atmosphere of his studio was self-consciously bohemian; he painted it bright chrome yellow and decorated it with primitive objects which he believed recalled 'a naval officer's *pied-à-terre* or the home to which an explorer now and then returns'. Here Gauguin hosted a number of gatherings attended by artists and literary figures.

In the spring of 1894 Gauguin and Annah visited Brittany together, and after some sailors spoke rudely to her Gauguin became involved in a brawl. One of the sailors kicked him with his wooden clog and broke Gauguin's ankle. While he was laid up in hospital and unable to paint, Annah returned to Paris, ransacked the studio, and disappeared without a trace.

By the winter of 1894-95 Gauguin was planning his second trip to Tahiti and applied unsuccessfully for a French administrative post in Oceania. His attempts to sell a number of paintings to the state also failed and a second auction sale at the Hôtel Drouot in February 1895 barely made a profit. Nevertheless at the beginning of July Gauguin left France for the last time, bound for Tahiti. Wasting no time in Papeete (which he noted in a letter to the composer William Molard was now lit by electricity), he traveled on to Punaauia, a small village on the west coast of the island. Here he constructed a

RIGHT: Detail from the *Papyrus of Ani (Theban Book of the Dead)*. Egyptian. 19th Dynasty. A photograph of this was one of the many elements that Gauguin used in Tahiti to give his work an authentic 'primitive' flavor.

native hut and found yet another female companion, the fourteen-year-old Pahura, who bore him two children.

Constantly painting and busy with illustrations for *Noa Noa*, Gauguin was still beset by material and bodily worries. His health was failing, due to syphilis contracted from a Montparnasse prostitute during his last stay in Paris, and his broken ankle had not healed properly. Furthermore, he was in debt to the *Caisse Agricole*, the bank of Tahiti. At this particularly trying period came news of his daughter Aline's death, and in 1897 Gauguin attempted suicide — but only after he had completed his most definitive artistic statement, the huge canvas *Where do we come from? What are we? Where are we going?*

To make ends meet, Gauguin took a clerk's job at the Public Works Office in Papeete, earning six francs a day. At the end of the year, when he returned to his hut in Punaauia, he found it in pieces, ravaged by rats, roaches and rainstorms. To take his mind off his troubles, Gauguin launched a newspaper, handwritten and copied on a stencilling machine. *Le Sourire, Journal Méchant* contained some of his finest woodcuts and brought him in a little money. But the newspaper was not to occupy him for long and again he was restless: in 1901 he wrote to Charles Morice:

I'm at the end of my rope . . . I'm going to make one final effort and am off next month to Fatu-Iua in the Marquesas, an island still almost cannibalistic. I think that the savage element there, together with complete solitude, will revive my fire of enthusiasm before I die . . .

In August 1901, Gauguin left Tahiti for Hiva-oa, one of the smaller of the Marquesas Islands, some 700 miles

north-east of Tahiti. He settled the following month in the large village of Atuana. The location was ideal: on one side was the open sea and the beach which would appear as the pink sand of *Riders on the Beach*, while on the other side was the mysterious valley, the setting for *Three Women and White Horse*. Gauguin called his bungalow home in the village 'La Maison du Jouir' and carved the name above the door. He soon found another fourteen-year-old girlfriend to live with him and bear his last child. But his health was becoming progressively worse and he was embroiled in conflict with local missionaries and the Bishop, who expressed concern over his 'paganism'. For a time Gauguin seriously considered returning to France. Monfreid, in a letter to Gauguin in December 1902, advised him against the journey.

You would do best not to come back . . . You now enjoy the immunity of the honored dead . . . Your name has passed into art history.

In March 1903 Gauguin was sentenced to three months in prison and a fine of 1000 francs for defaming a member of the local police force. He appealed against the sentence and the appeal was being heard when, on 8 May, sensing the end, Gauguin asked an old Maori friend, Tioka, to fetch a Protestant missionary, Pastor Vernier, who had been more favorably disposed toward Gauguin than the Catholic establishment. After a few comforting words, Vernier left the house. When he returned later that day, he found Gauguin dead. Tioka pronounced his epitaph to Gauguin's native friends: 'Now he is a man no longer.'

Landscape, 1873
Oil on canvas, 19⅞×32⅛ inches (50.5×81.6 cm)
The Norton Simon Foundation. Pasadena. California

The Market Gardens at Vaugirard, 1879
Oil on canvas, 25½×39⅜ inches (65×100 cm)
Smith College Museum of Art, Northampton, Massachusetts

Study of a Nude or Suzanne Sewing, 1880
Oil on canvas, 45¼×31½ inches (115×80 cm)
Ny Carlsberg Glyptotek, Copenhagen

Flowers and Cats, 1889
Oil on canvas, 36⅕×28¼ inches (93.4×72.3 cm)
Ny Carlsberg Glyptotek, Copenhagen

ABOVE
Garden in the Rue Carcel, 1881-2
Oil on canvas, 34¼×44⅞ inches (87×114 cm)
Ny Carlsberg Glyptotek, Copenhagen

RIGHT
Madame Mette Gauguin, 1884
Oil on canvas, 25½×21¼ inches (65×54 cm)
National Gallery, Oslo

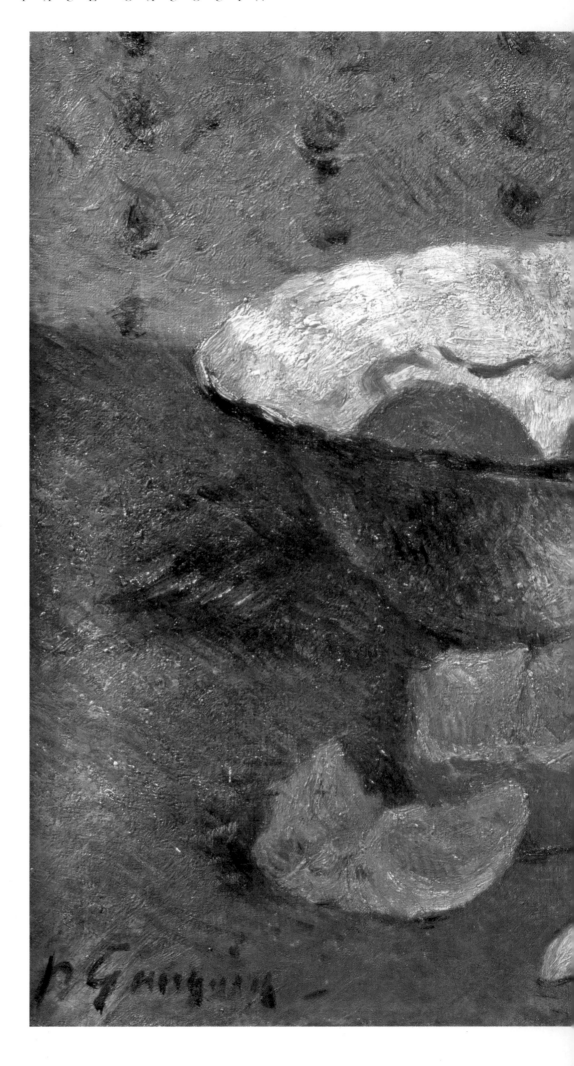

Still Life with Oranges, c.1881
*Oil on canvas, 13×18¼ inches
(33×46 cm)*
Musée des Beaux-Arts, Rennes

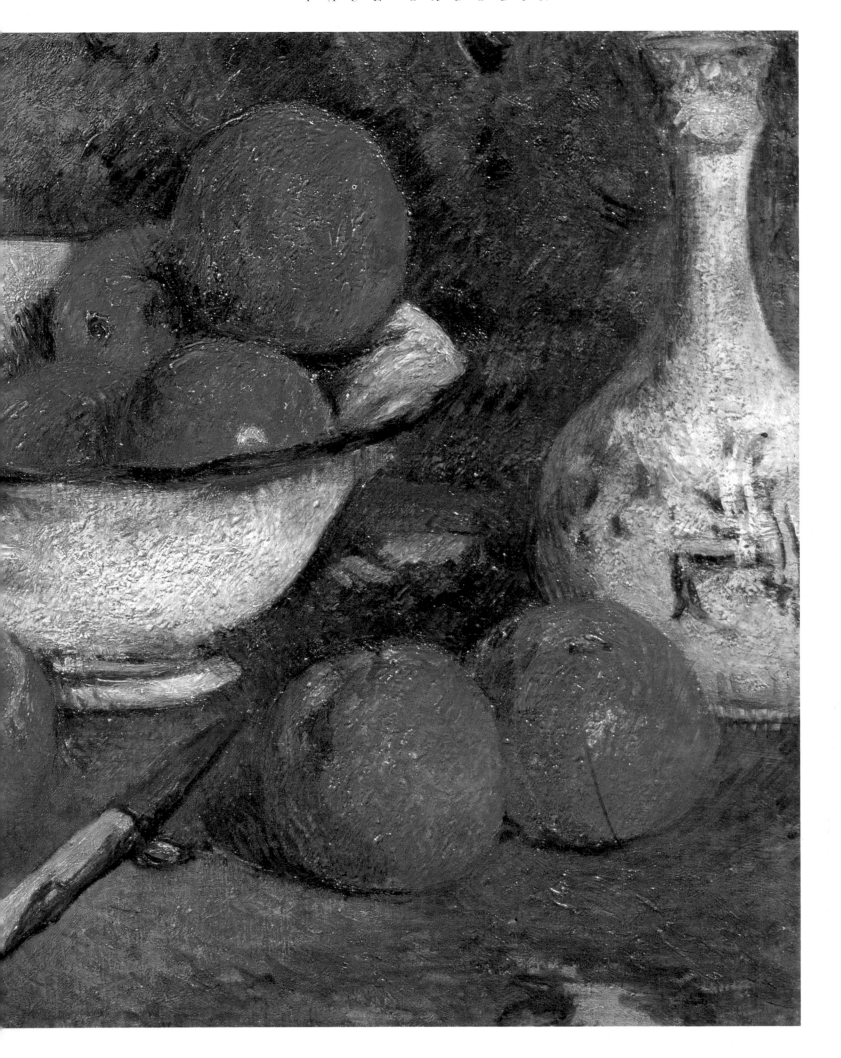

Entrance to a Village, 1884
Oil on canvas, 23½×28¾ inches (59.5×73 cm)
Museum of Fine Arts, Boston

Sleeping Child, 1884
Oil on canvas, 18⅛×21⅞ inches (46×55.5 cm)
Josefowitz Collection

Oestervold Park, Copenhagen, 1885
Oil on canvas, 23¼×28¾ inches (59×73 cm)
Glasgow Museums: Art Gallery and Museums, Kelvingrove

Still Life with Mandolin, 1885
Oil on canvas, 24×20 inches (61×51 cm)
Musée d'Orsay, Paris

34

Women Bathing, 1885
Oil on canvas, 15×18¼ inches (38.1×46.2 cm)
National Museum of Western Art, Tokyo

The Breton Shepherdess, 1886
Oil on canvas, 24×28 inches (61×73.5 cm)
Laing Art Gallery, Newcastle-upon-Tyne

Four Breton Women, 1886
Oil on canvas, 28⅜×35⅜ inches
(72×90 cm)
Bayerischen Staatsgemäl-
desammlungen, Munich

LEFT
Still Life with Profile of Laval, 1886
Oil on canvas, 18⅛×15 inches (46×38 cm)
Josefowitz Collection

ABOVE
Martinique Landscape, 1887
Oil on canvas, 45¾×35 inches (115.5×89 cm)
National Gallery of Scotland, Edinburgh

By the Sea, Martinique, 1887
Oil on canvas, 21¼×35½ inches (54×90 cm)
Ny Carlsberg Glyptotek, Copenhagen

**Breton Girls Dancing,
Pont-Aven,** 1888
*Oil on canvas, 28¾×36½ inches
(73×92.7 cm)*
National Gallery of Art, Washington

LEFT
Boys Wrestling, 1888
Oil on canvas, 36⅝×28¾ inches (93×73 cm)
Josefowitz Collection

ABOVE
Landscape of Bretagne, 1888
Oil on canvas, 35½×28 inches (90.9×71.7 cm)
Ny Carlsberg Glyptotek, Copenhagen

48

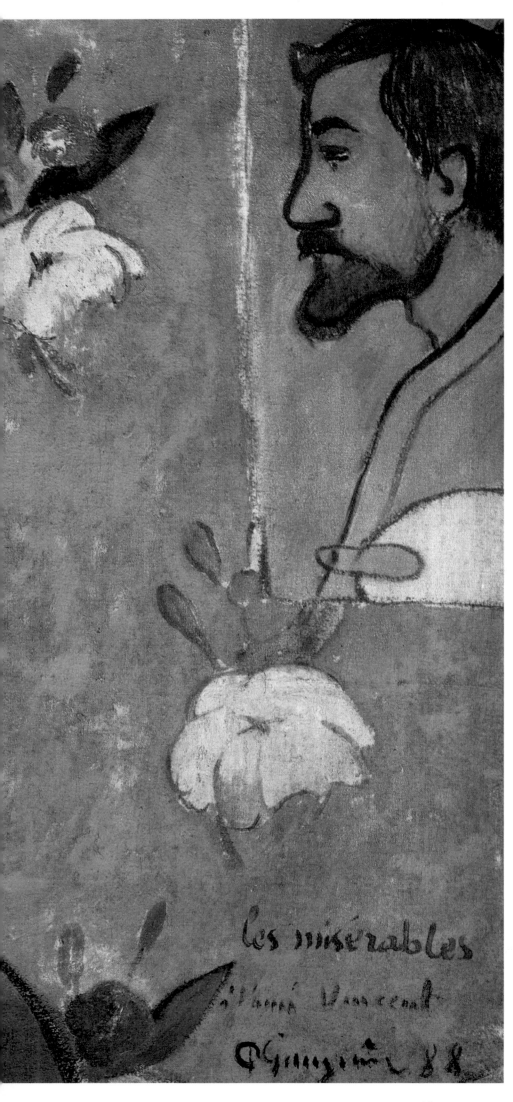

les misérables

Gauguin 88

Self-Portrait (Les Misérables), 1888
*Oil on canvas, 17³/₄×21⁵/₈ inches
(45×55 cm)*
National Museum Vincent Van Gogh,
Amsterdam

49

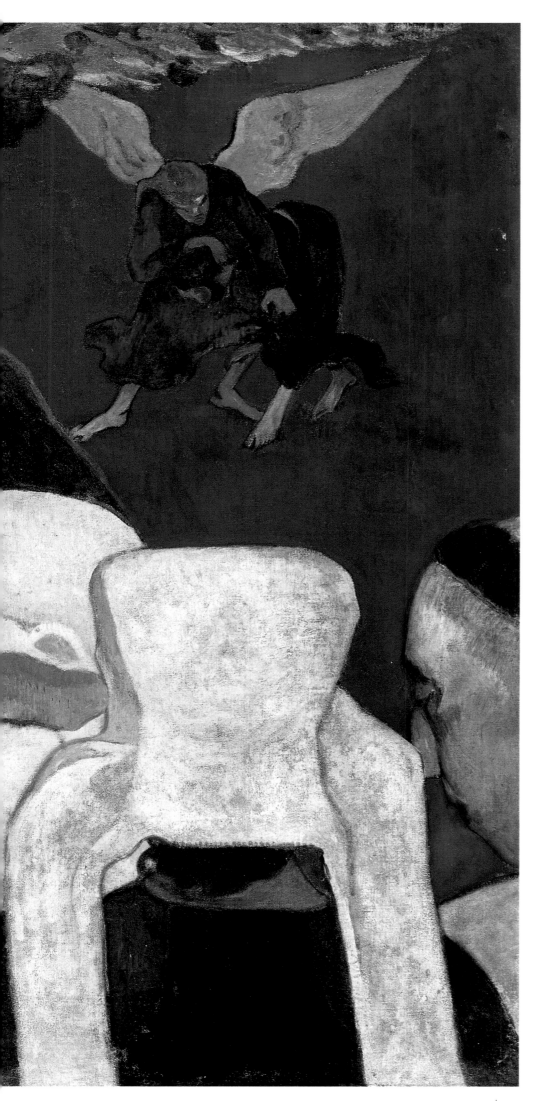

**Vision after the Sermon or Jacob
Wrestling with the Angel**, 1888
*Oil on canvas, 28¾×36¼ inches
(73×92 cm)*
National Gallery of Scotland

Portrait of Madeleine Bernard, 1889
Oil on canvas, 28³/₈×22³/₄ inches (72×58 cm)
Musée de Grenoble

Still Life, Fête Gloanec, 1888
Oil on canvas, 15×20⅞ inches (38×53 cm)
Musée des Beaux-Arts, Orléans

ABOVE
Old Women at Arles, 1888
Oil on canvas, 28¾×36¼ inches (73×92 cm)
Art Institute of Chicago

LEFT
Young Bretons Bathing, 1888
Oil on canvas, 36¼×28¾ inches (92×73 cm)
Kunsthalle, Hamburg

Van Gogh Painting Sunflowers, 1888
*Oil on canvas, 28¾×36¼ inches
(73×92 cm)*
National Museum Vincent Van Gogh,
Amsterdam

Night Café at Arles (Madame Ginoux), 1888
*Oil on canvas, 28³/₄×36¹/₄ inches
(73×92 cm)*
Pushkin Museum, Moscow

The Alyscamps, 1888
Oil on canvas, 36¼×28¾ inches (92×73 cm)
Musée d'Orsay, Paris

Landscape near Arles, 1888
Oil on canvas, 36×28½ inches (91×72 cm)
Museum of Art, Indianapolis

Grape Harvest at Arles, Human Anguish, 1888
*Oil on canvas, 28¾×36¼ inches
(73×92 cm)*
Ordrupgaard Collection, Copenhagen

Still Life with Fan, 1889
Oil on canvas, 19¾×24 inches (50×61 cm)
Musée d'Orsay, Paris

La Belle Angèle, 1889
Oil on canvas, 36¾×28¾ inches (92×73 cm)
Musée d'Orsay, Paris

Bonjour Monsieur Gauguin, 1889
Oil on canvas, 44½×36¼ inches (113×92 cm)
National Gallery, Prague

Nirvana, Portrait of Meyer de Haan, 1889
Essence on silk, 8×11½ inches (20×29 cm)
Wadsworth Atheneum, Hartford

70

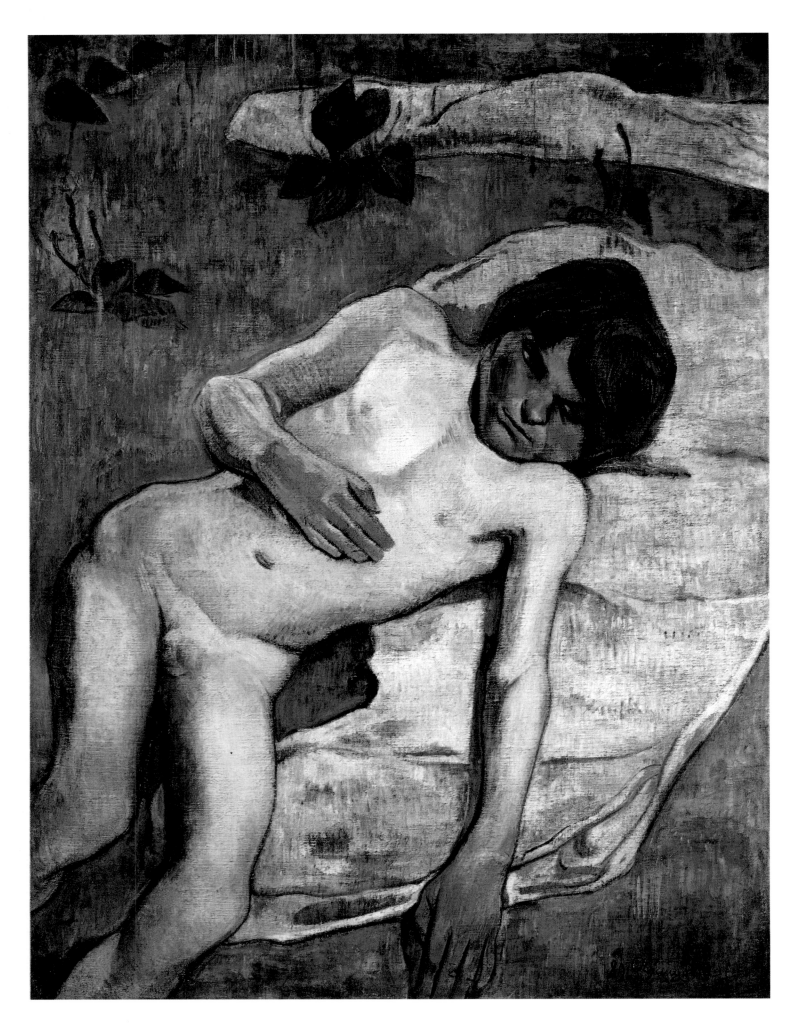

Self-Portrait with Halo, 1889
Oil on wood, 31¾×20¼ inches (79.2×51.3 cm)
National Gallery of Art, Washington

Naked Breton Boy, 1889
Oil on canvas, 36⅝×29 inches (93×73.5 cm)
Wallraf-Richartz Museum, Cologne

ABOVE
Yellow Haystacks, 1889
Oil on canvas, 29×36⅝ inches (73.5×93 cm)
Musée d'Orsay, Paris

LEFT
Woman in the Waves (Ondine), 1889
Oil on canvas, 36¼×28⅜ inches (92×72 cm)
Cleveland Museum of Art

Yellow Christ, 1889
Oil on canvas, 36¼×28¾ inches (92×73 cm)
Albright-Knox Art Gallery, Buffalo

Green Christ (Breton Calvary), 1889
Oil on canvas, 36¼×28¾ inches (92×73 cm)
Musées Royaux des Beaux-Arts de Belgique, Brussels

ABOVE
Landscape at Le Pouldu, 1890
Oil on canvas, 28⅞×36⅜ inches (73.3×92.4 cm)
National Gallery of Art, Washington

LEFT
Haymaking, 1889
Oil on canvas, 36¼×28¾ inches (92×73 cm)
Courtauld Institute Galleries, London

The Loss of Virginity or The Awakening of Spring, 1890
Oil on canvas, 35½×51¼ inches (90×130 cm)
Chrysler Museum, Norfolk, Virginia

ABOVE
**Portrait of a Woman, with Still Life by
Cézanne**, 1890
Oil on canvas, 25¾×21⅝ inches (65.3×54.9 cm)
Art Institute of Chicago

RIGHT
Te Faaturuma (Melancholic), 1891
Oil on canvas, 36⅕×28¾ inches (92.7×73.6 cm)
William Rockhill Nelson Collection in the Nelson Gallery,
Kansas City, Missouri (38.5)

Tahitian Landscape, 1891
Oil on canvas, 26¾×36⅜ inches (68×92 cm)
Minneapolis Institute of Arts

84

Suzanne Bambridge, 1891
Oil on canvas, 27½×19¾ inches (70×50 cm)
Musées Royeaux des Beaux-Arts de Belgique, Brussels

Portrait of the Artist with the Idol, 1891
Oil on canvas, 18×13⅝ inches (46×33 cm)
Marion Koogler McNay Art Institute, San Antonio, Texas

The Meal, 1891
*Oil on canvas, 28⅞×36⅜ inches
(73×92 cm)*
Musée d'Orsay, Paris

**Women of Tahiti: On the
Beach,** 1891
*Oil on canvas, 27⅛×35½ inches
(69×90 cm)*
Musée d'Orsay, Paris

IA ORANA MARIA

ABOVE
Te Tiare Farani (The Flowers of France), 1891
Oil on canvas, 28³⁄₈×36¹⁄₄ inches (72×92 cm)
Hermitage Museum, Leningrad

LEFT
Ia Orana Maria (Hail Mary), 1891
Oil on canvas, 44³⁄₄×34¹⁄₂ inches (113.7×87.7 cm)
Metropolitan Museum of Art, New York

Man with an Ax, 1891
Oil on canvas, 36¼×27½ inches (92×70 cm)
Private Collection

Tahitian Landscape with Four Figures, 1892
Oil on canvas, 35⅛×27⅜ inches (90×70 cm)
Ny Carlsberg Glyptotek, Copenhagen

Aha oe Feii? (What! Are you jealous?), 1892
*Oil on canvas, 26×35 inches
(66.6×89.6 cm)*
Moscow, Pushkin Museum

LEFT

Vahine no te Vi (Woman with a Mango), 1892
Oil on canvas, 28⅝×17½ inches (72.7×44.5 cm)
Baltimore Museum of Art

ABOVE

Parau na te Varua ino (Words of the Devil), 1892
Oil on canvas, 36⅛×27 inches (91.7×68.5 cm)
National Gallery of Art, Washington

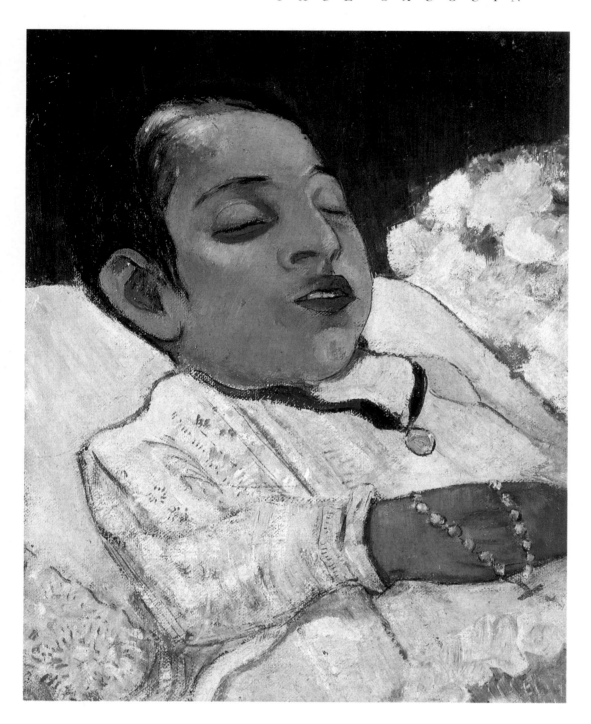

ABOVE
Portrait of Atiti, 1892
Oil on canvas, 11¾×9¾ inches (30×25 cm)
State Museum Kröller-Müller, Otterlo

RIGHT
Nafea Faa Ipoipo (When will you Marry?), 1892
Oil on canvas, 40×30½ inches (101.5×77.5 cm)
Rudolf Staechelin Foundation, Basle

Manao Tupapau (The Spirit of the Dead keeps Watch), 1892
*Oil on burlap mounted on canvas,
28½×36⅜ inches (73×92 cm)*
Albright-Knox Art Gallery, Buffalo

Arearea (Pranks), 1892
Oil on canvas, 29½×37 inches
(75×94 cm)
Musée d'Orsay, Paris

ABOVE
Ta Matete (The Market), 1892
Tempera on canvas, 28¾×36¼ inches (73×92 cm)
Kunstmuseum, Basle

RIGHT
**Merahi Metua no Tehamana
(The Ancestors of Tehamana),** 1893
Oil on canvas, 30×21⅜ inches (76.3×54.3 cm)
Art Institute of Chicago

ABOVE
Pape Moe (Mysterious Water), 1893
Oil on canvas, 39×29½ inches (99×75 cm)
Private Collection, Switzerland

Ea Haere Ia Oe? (Where are you Going?), 1893
Oil on canvas, 35¾×28 inches (91×71 cm)
Hermitage Museum, Leningrad

Self-Portrait Wearing a Hat, 1893
Oil on canvas, 18⅛×15 inches (46×38 cm)
Musée d'Orsay, Paris

Mahana no Atua (Day of the God), 1894
Oil on canvas, 26⅞×36 inches (68.3×91.5 cm)
Art Institute of Chicago

Peasant Women from Brittany, 1894
Oil on canvas, 23⅝×36¼ inches (60×92 cm)
Musée d'Orsay, Paris

111

Upaupa Schneklud, 1894
Oil on canvas, 36½×28⅞ inches (92.5×73.5 cm)
Baltimore Museum of Art

Self-Portrait (at Golgotha), 1896
Oil on canvas, 30×37 inches (76×94 cm)
Museu de Arte, São Paulo

Te Tamari no Atua (The Birth of Christ, Son of God), 1896
Oil on canvas, 37¾×50¾ inches (96×129 cm)
Bayerische Staatsgemäldesammlungen, Munich

115

Where do we come from? What are we? Where are we going?, 1897
Oil on canvas, 54¾×147½ inches (139.1×374.6 cm)
Museum of Fine Arts, Boston

Three Tahitians, 1899
Oil on canvas, 28¾×36 inches (73×91 cm)
National Gallery of Scotland

And the Gold of their Bodies, 1901
Oil on canvas, 26³/₈×31¹/₈ inches (67×79 cm)
Musée d'Orsay, Paris

Still Life with Sunflowers, 1901
Oil on canvas, 26×30 inches (66×76 cm)
Private Collection, Switzerland

ABOVE
Riders on the Beach, 1902
Oil on canvas, 26×28 inches (66×76 cm)
Folkwang Museum, Essen

LEFT
Girl with a Fan, 1902
Oil on canvas, 36¼×28¾ inches (92×73 cm)
Folkwang Museum, Essen

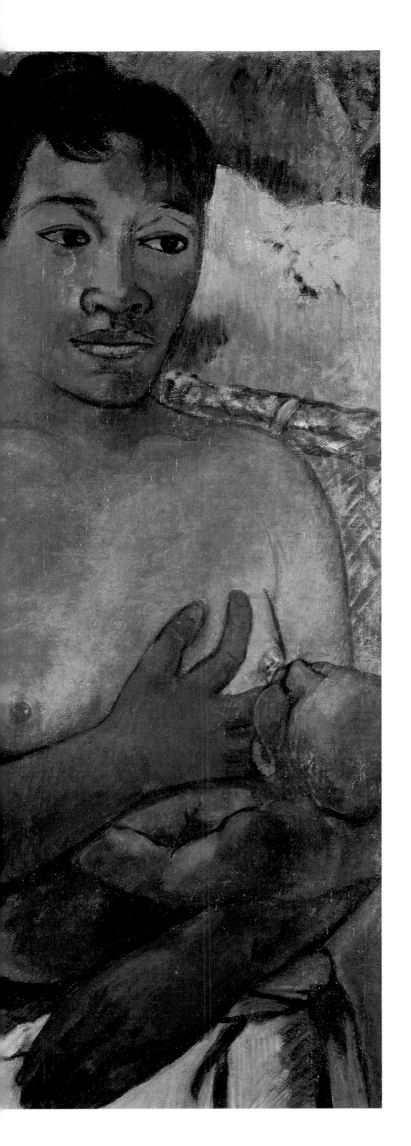

The Offering, 1902
Oil on canvas, 27×31 inches (68.6×78.7 cm)
Foundation E G Bührle Collection, Zürich, Switzerland

125

Contes Barbares (Primitive Tales), 1902
Oil on canvas, 51¾×35⅝ inches (131.5×90.5 cm)
Folkwang Museum, Essen

Landscape with a Pig and a Horse, 1902
Oil on canvas, 29¼×25⅜ inches (75×65 cm)
Art Museum of the Ateneum, Helsinki

ACKNOWLEDGMENTS

The publisher would like to thank Martin Bristow, who designed this book; Jessica Hodge, the editor; and Veronica Price, the production manager. We would also like to thank the following institutions and agencies for the loan of photographic material.

Albright-Knox Art Gallery, Buffalo/Bridgeman Art Library: pages 74, 100-101 (A Conger Goodyear Collection 1965)

The Art Institute of Chicago: pages 55 (Mr and Mrs Lewis Larned Coburn Memorial Collection, 1934.391), 81 (The Joseph Winterbotham Collection, 1925.753), 105 (Gift of Mr and Mrs Charles Deering McCormick, 1980.613), 109 (Helen Birch Bartlett Memorial Collection, 1926.198)

Art Museum of the Ateneum, Helsinki: page 127

Baltimore Museum of Art: pages 96 (The Cone Collection, formed by Dr Claribel Cone and Miss Etta Cone of Baltimore, Maryland), 112 (Given by Hilda K Blaustein in memory of her husband Jakob Blaustein)

British Museum/photo C M Dixon: page 17

Burrell Collection, Glasgow Museums and Art Galleries: page 9

Chrysler Museum, Norfolk, VA: pages 78-79

Cleveland Museum of Art: page 72 (Gift of Mr and Mrs William Powell Jones, 78.63)

Collection Viollet: pages 11, 15, 16

Courtauld Institute Galleries, London (Courtauld Collection): pages 10 (top), 76

Fitzwilliam Museum, Cambridge, UK: pages 18-19

Folkwang Museum, Essen: pages 122, 123, 126

Foundation E G Bührle Collection, Zurich/photo W Drayer: pages 120-121, 124-125

Giraudon/Weidenfeld Archive page 7

Glasgow Art Gallery and Museums: page 32

Hermitage Museum, Leningrad/photo SCALA: pages 91, 107

Hulton-Deutsch Collection, London: page 6

Indianapolis Museum of Art: page 61 (Fift in Memory of William Ray Adams)

Josefowitz Collection: pages 14, 30-31, 40, 46

Kunsthalle, Hamburg: page 54

Kunstmuseum, Basle: page 104

Laing Art Gallery, Newcastle-upon-Tyne, reproduced by permission of Tyne and Wear Museums Services: pages 36-37

Marion Koogler McNay Institute, San Antonio, Texas: page 85 (Bequest of Marion Koogler McNay, 1950.46)

Metropolitan Museum of Art, New York: page 90 (Bequest of Sam A Lewinsohn 1951, 51.112.2)

Minneapolis Institute of Arts: pages 82-83 (The Julius C Eliel Memorial Fund)

Musée d'Albi: page 13

Musée de Grenoble: page 52

Musée des Beaux-Arts, Orléans: page 53

Musée des Beaux-Arts, Rennes/Bridgeman Art Library: pages 26-27

Musée d'Orsay/Photo RMN: pages 33, 60, 65, 66, 73, 86-87, 88-89, 102-103, 108, 110-111, 119

Musée Marmottan, Paris/Bridgeman Art Library: page 10 (bottom)

Musées royaux d'Art et d'Histoire, Brussels: page 12 (top)

Musées royaux des Beaux-Arts de Belgique, Brussels: pages 75, 84

Museu de Arte de São Paulo, Brazil: page 112

Courtesy Museum of Fine Arts, Boston: pages 28-29 (Bequest of John T Spaulding), 116-117 (Tompkins Collection Purchase, Arthur Gordon Tompkins Fund 1936)

National Gallery, London: page 8

National Gallery, Oslo/photo Jacques Lathion: page 25

National Gallery, Prague: page 67

National Gallery of Art, Washington: pages 44-45, 70 (Chester Dale Collection), 77 (Collection of Mr and Mrs Paul Mellon), 97 (Gift of the W Averell Harriman Foundation in memory of Marie N Harriman)

National Gallery of Scotland, Edinburgh: pages 41, 50-51, 118

National Museum of Western Art, Tokyo, Matsukata Collection: pages 34-35

Nelson-Atkins Museum of Art, Kansas City: page 81

Neue Pinakothek, Munich/photo Artothek: pages 38-39, 114-115

Ny Carlesberg Glyptotek, Copenhagen: pages 22, 23, 24, 42-43/Bridgeman Art Library, 47, 93

Ordrupgaard Collection, Copenhagen: pages 62-63

Private Collection: page 92

Private Collection, Switzerland: page 106

Pushkin Museum, Moscow/photo SCALA: pages 58-59, 94-95

Rudolph Staechelin Family Foundation, Basle/colorphoto Hans Hinz: page 99

Smith College Museum of Art, Northampton, Mass: pages 20-21

State Museum Kröller-Müller, Otterlo: page 98

Vincent Van Gogh Foundation/National Museum Vincent Van Gogh, Amsterdam: pages 48-49, 56-57

Wadsworth Atheneum, Hartford, CT: pages 68-69 (Ella Gallup Sumner and Mary Catlin Sumner Collection)

Wallraf-Richartz Museum, Cologne: page 71

Yale University Art Gallery: page 12 (bottom) (Bequest of Stephen Carlton Clark BA, 1903)